Krönungshymnen

für

König Georg II.

von

Georg Friedrich Händel.

Ausgabe der Deutschen Händelgesellschaft.

Four Coronation Anthems

in Full Score

Composed for the Coronation of King George II
Westminster Abbey, 11 October 1727

George Frideric
HANDEL

DOVER PUBLICATIONS, INC.
Mineola, New York

Bibliographical Note

This Dover edition, first published in 1999, is an unabridged republication of *Krönungshymnen für König Georg II* from *Georg Friedrich Händel's Werke / Ausgabe der Deutßchen Händelgeßellßhaft*, edited by Friedrich Chrysander, originally published by Breitkopf & Härtel, Leipzig, n.d. [1863]. The instrumentation list and footnote are newly added.

We are indebted to the Sibley Music Library, Eastman School of Music, for making this score available to us.

International Standard Book Number: 0-486-40627-X

Manufactured in the United States of America
Dover Publications, Inc., 31 East 2nd Street, Mineola, N.Y. 11501

Coronation Anthems.

Contents.

Krönungshymnen.

Inhalt.

PREFACE.

The coronation for which Handel composed the four following hymns, took place at Westminster Abbey on the 11th September 1727. The order of the festival, the arrangement of the choruses, &c., will be found fully described in my Life of Handel, II. 170—74. As there is no close connexion between these four separate anthems, and the order in which they succeeded one another at the original festivity cannot be determined with certainty, the editor must be guided by considerations of propriety in arranging them. Handel began with the composition of *Zadok the priest,* which should always stand first; and ended with that of the anthem to the Queen, *My heart is inditing.* In his manuscript they have now this order, 1. 3. 4. 2; but in Smith's transcript this, 4. 2. 3. 1. In Arnold's edition they stand thus, 4. 2. 1. 3; and in the edition of the former Handel Society thus, 2. 1. 3. 4. But our agreement agrees best with the requirements both of Handel's music and of the service.

The texts are frequently noted by Handel at the commencement of the pieces. In *Zadok the priest:* "1 Kings I. 48" [it should be 39 and 40]. In *The King shall rejoice:* "Ψ 45. V. 1. 10.12. [*Prayer Book Version.*] Ψ [read *Isaiah*] 49. V. 23." In the anthem *Let thy hand be strengthened,* taken from the 89th Psalm, the text is not noted.

In the *Allelujah* Handel often, in Italian fashion, blends the last syllable of one word with the first of the following: *Alleluj' Allelujah.* The English editions, by not observing this, have given to the words a false rhythm at this place.

The pianoforte arrangement of the present edition is by Im. Faisst.

LEIPZIG, January 1, 1863.

Chr.

INSTRUMENTATION

Listed in modern score order

2 Oboes [Oboe]
2 Bassoons [Fagotto]

3 Trumpets in C [Tromba]

Timpani [Timpani]

Violins I, II, III [Violino]
Viola [Viola]
Cellos & Basses [Violoncelli e Contrabassi]

Organ *(continuo)** [Organo]

Full Chorus of Mixed Voices:
SSAATBB

Keyboard reduction** [Pianoforte]

*For a detailed discussion of Handel's orchestra, and especially of continuo practice in works of this nature—including use of the positive organ and harpsichord—see Paul Henry Lang's *George Frideric Handel,* Chapter XXVI (Dover, 1996: 0-486-29227-4).

**Friedrich Chrysander ["Chr."]—founder of the Handel-Gesellschaft and editor of this volume—added the pianoforte part in the form of a keyboard reduction and realization.

Four Coronation Anthems

in Full Score

ANTHEM 1.

ZADOK THE PRIEST.
Zadok der Priester.

9

and all the peo-ple re-joic'd, _____ re-joic'd, re-joic'd,

und al-les Volk rings froh-lockt', _____ froh-lockt', froh-lockt',

and all the peo-ple re-joic'd, _____ re-joic'd, re-joic'd,

und al-les Volk rings froh-lockt', _____ froh-lockt', froh-lockt',

and all the peo-ple re-joic'd, _____ re-joic'd, re-joic'd,

12

peo_ple re _ joic'd, _____ re _ joic'd, re _ joic'd, and said:

Volk rings froh _ lockt', _____ *froh _ lockt', froh _ lockt', und rief:*

peo_ple re _ joic'd, _____ re _ joic'd, re _ joic'd, and said:

Volk rings froh _ lockt', _____ *froh _ lockt', froh _ lockt', und rief:*

peo_ple re _ joic'd, _____ re _ joic'd, re _ joic'd, and said:

Adagio.

14

_ _ _ _ _ men! A_men! A_men! Al_le _ lu_ja, A _ men!

_ _ _ _ _ men! A_men! A_men! Al_le _ lu_ja, A _ men!

_ _ _ _ _ men! A_men! A_men! Al_le _ lu_ja, A _ men!

_ _ _ _ _ men! A_men! A_men! Al_le _ lu_ja, A _ men!

_ _ _ _ _ men! A_men! A_men! Al_le _ lu_ja, A _ men!

Violoncelli.

6   6 7 6   6   4   6
                        2

God save the King,

Gott sei dein Schild,

God save the King,

Gott sei dein Schild,

God save the King,

Gott sei dein Schild,

God save the King,

Gott sei dein Schild,

Tutti, forte.

ff

ev_er, for ev_er, A_men, A_men, Al_le_lu_ja, Al_le _ lu_ja, A _ men! A _ _ _ _ _ _ _
e_wig, auf e_wig,

ev _ _ _ er, A_men, A_men, Al_le_lu_ja, Al_le _ lu_ja, A _ men! A _ _ _ _ _ _ _
e _ _ _ wig,

ev _ _ _ er, A_men, A_men, Al_le_lu_ja, Al_le _ lu_ja, A _ men! A _ _ _ _ _ _ _
e _ _ _ wig,

ev_er, for ev_er, A_men, A_men, Al_le_lu_ja, Al_le _ lu_ja, A _ men! A _ _ _ _ _ _ _
e_wig, auf e_wig,

ev_er, for ev_er, A_men, A_men, Al_le_lu_ja, Al_le _ lu_ja, A_men! A _ _ _ _ _ _ _

e_wig, auf e_wig, A_men, A_men, Al_le_lu_ja, Al_le _ lu_ja, A _ men! A _ _ _ _ _ _ _

Adagio.

Amen, Amen, Alle_lu_ja, A_men, Alle_lu_ja, A_men, Amen, Al_le_lu_ja, Al_le_lu_ja!

Amen, Amen, Alle_lu_ja, A_men, Alle_lu_ja, A_men, Amen, Al_le_lu_ja, Al_le_lu_ja!

Amen, Amen, Alle_lu_ja, A_men, Alle_lu_ja, A_men, Amen, Al_le_lu_ja, Al_le_lu_ja!

Amen, Amen, Alle_lu_ja, A_men, Alle_lu_ja, A_men, Amen, Al_le_lu_ja, Al_le_lu_ja!

Amen, Amen, Alle_lu_ja, A_men, Alle_lu_ja, A_men, Amen, Al_le_lu_ja, Al_le_lu_ja!

Amen, Amen, Alle_lu_ja, A_men, Alle_lu_ja, A_men, Amen, Al_le_lu_ja, Al_le_lu_ja!

Adagio.

P.

ANTHEM 2.

THE KING SHALL REJOICE.

Der Fürst wird sich freu'n.

31

The King shall re-joice, the King shall re-joice in thy strength, oh

Der Fürst wird sich freu'n, der Fürst wird sich freu'n deiner Macht, o

The King shall re-joice, the King shall re-joice in thy strength, oh

Der Fürst wird sich freu'n, der Fürst wird sich freu'n deiner Macht, o

The King shall re-joice, the King shall re-joice in thy strength, oh

Der Fürst wird sich freu'n, der Fürst wird sich freu'n deiner Macht, o

Lord! ... the King shall re-joice, shall re-joice,_____

Herr! ... der Fürst wird sich freu'n, wird sich freu'n,_____

Lord! ... the King shall re-joice, shall re-joice,_____

Herr! ... der Fürst wird sich freu'n, wird sich freu'n,_____

Lord! ... the King shall re-joice, shall re-joice_____

Herr! ... der Fürst wird sich freu'n, wird sich freu'n _____

the King shall re_joice in thy strength, oh Lord!
der Fürst wird sich freu'n deiner Macht, o Herr!

the King shall re_joice in thy strength, oh Lord!
der Fürst wird sich freu'n deiner Macht, o Herr!

the King shall re_joice in thy strength, oh Lord!
der Fürst wird sich freu'n deiner Macht, o Herr!

the King shall re_
der König wird sich

der Fürst wird sich

the King shall re_
der Fürst wird sich

the King shall re_
der König wird sich

37

44

tion.

de.

tion.

de.

51

and hast set a crown of pure gold___ up_on his head.

und hast mit der Kron' rei_nen Gold's ge_krönt sein Haupt.

and hast set a crown of pure gold up_on his head.

und hast mit der Kron' rei_nen Gold's ge_krönt sein Haupt.

and hast set a crown of pure gold up_on his head.

und hast mit der Kron' rei_nen Gold's ge_krönt sein Haupt.

dim.

Al _le_lu _ ja!   Al _ le_lu _ ja,

Al_le _ lu _ ja, _____ Al _le _ lu _ ja!   Al _ le_lu _ ja,Alle _ lu _ ja,_____ Al_le _ lu _

Al_le _ lu _ ja, _____ Al _le _ lu _ ja!   Al _ le _ lu _ ja,   Al _ le _ luja,_____

Al_le_lu _ ja,_____ Al _ le_lu _ ja! Al_le _ lu_ja, _____ Al _ le _ lu _ ja, Al _ le _ _ lu _

Al_le_lu _ ja,   Al _ le _ lu _ ja! Al _le_lu _ ja,   Al _ le_lu _ ja,_____

Al_le_lu _ ja,   Al _ le _ lu _ ja!   Al _ le_lu _ ja,_____

Organo tasto solo.

ANTHEM 3.

MY HEART IS INDITING.

Mein Herz denkt und dichtet.

77

which I have made — un_to the King.

das ich be_stimmt für meinen Herrn.

which I have made un _ to the King.

das ich be_stimmt für meinen Herrn.

which I have made un _ to the King.

das ich be_stimmt für mei _ nen Herrn.

82

94

ANTHEM 4.

LET THY HAND BE STRENGTHENED.

Deine Hand erstarke.

121

125

(con Oboi.)

Dover Opera, Choral and Lieder Scores

LOHENGRIN IN FULL SCORE, Richard Wagner. Wagner's most accessible opera. Reproduced from first engraved edition (Breitkopf & Härtel, 1887). 295pp. 9⅜ × 12¼. 24335-4 Pa. **$19.95**

TANNHAUSER IN FULL SCORE, Richard Wagner. Reproduces the original 1845 full orchestral and vocal score as slightly amended in 1847. Included is the ballet music for Act I written for the 1861 Paris production. 576pp. 8⅜ × 11¼. 24649-3 Pa. **$23.95**

TRISTAN UND ISOLDE, Richard Wagner. Full orchestral score with complete instrumentation. Study score. 655pp. 8¼ × 11. 22915-7 Pa. **$24.95**

PARSIFAL IN FULL SCORE, Richard Wagner. Composer's deeply personal treatment of the legend of the Holy Grail, renowned for splendid music, glowing orchestration. C. F. Peters edition. 592pp. 8½ × 11. 25175-6 Pa. **$24.95**

THE FLYING DUTCHMAN IN FULL SCORE, Richard Wagner. Great early masterpiece reproduced directly from limited Weingartner edition (1896), incorporating Wagner's revisions. Text, stage directions in English, German, Italian. 432pp. 9⅜ × 12¼. 25629-4 Pa. **$22.95**

BORIS GODUNOV IN FULL SCORE (Rimsky-Korsakov Version), Modest Petrovich Moussorgsky. Russian operatic masterwork in most recorded, performed version. Authoritative Moscow edition. 784pp. 8⅜ × 11¼. 25321-X Pa. **$32.95**

PELLÉAS ET MÉLISANDE IN FULL SCORE, Claude Debussy. Reprinted from the E. Fromont (1904) edition, this volume faithfully reproduces the full orchestral-vocal score of Debussy's sole and enduring opera masterpiece. 416pp. 9 × 12. (Available in U.S. only) 24825-9 Pa. **$18.95**

SALOME IN FULL SCORE, Richard Strauss. Atmospheric color predominates in basic 20th-century work. Definitive Fürstner score, now extremely rare. 352pp. 9⅜ × 12¼. (Available in U.S. only) 24208-0 Pa. **$18.95**

DER ROSENKAVALIER IN FULL SCORE, Richard Strauss. First inexpensive edition of great operatic masterpiece, reprinted complete and unabridged from rare, limited Fürstner edition (1910) approved by Strauss. 528pp. 9⅜ × 12¼. (Available in U.S. only) 25498-4 Pa. **$24.95**

DER ROSENKAVALIER: VOCAL SCORE, Richard Strauss. Inexpensive edition reprinted directly from original Fürstner (1911) edition of vocal score. Verbal text, vocal line and piano "reduction." 448pp. 8⅜ × 11¼. (Available in U.S only) 25501-8 Pa. **$18.95**

THE MERRY WIDOW: Complete Score for Piano and Voice in English, Franz Lehar. Complete score for piano and voice, reprinted directly from the first English translation (1907) published by Chappell & Co., London. 224pp. 8⅜ × 11¼. (Available in U.S. only) 24514-4 Pa. **$12.95**

THE AUTHENTIC GILBERT & SULLIVAN SONGBOOK, W. S. Gilbert, A. S. Sullivan. 92 songs, uncut, original keys, in piano renderings approved by Sullivan. 399pp. 9 × 12. 23482-7 Pa. **$16.95**

MADRIGALS: BOOK IV & V, Claudio Monteverdi. 39 finest madrigals with new English line-for-line literal translations of the poems facing the Italian text. 256pp. 8½ × 11. (Available in U.S. only) 25102-0 Pa. **$12.95**

COMPLETE SONG CYCLES, Franz Schubert. Complete piano, vocal music of *Die Schöne Müllerin, Die Winterreise, Schwanengesang.* Also Drinker English singing translations. Breitkopf & Härtel edition. 217pp. 9⅜ × 12¼. 22649-2 Pa. **$11.95**

SCHUBERT'S SONGS TO TEXTS BY GOETHE, Franz Schubert. Only one-volume edition of Schubert's Goethe songs from authoritative Breitkopf & Härtel edition, plus all revised versions. New prose translation of poems. 84 songs. 256pp. 9⅜ × 12¼. 23752-4 Pa. **$14.95**

59 FAVORITE SONGS, Franz Schubert. "Der Wanderer," "Ave Maria," "Hark, Hark, the Lark," and 56 other masterpieces of lieder reproduced from the Breitkopf & Härtel edition. 256pp. 9⅜ × 12¼. 24849-6 Pa. **$12.95**

SONGS FOR SOLO VOICE AND PIANO, Ludwig van Beethoven. 71 lieder, including "Adelaide," "Wonne der Wehmuth," "Die ehre Gottes aus der Natur," and famous cycle *An die ferne Geliebta.* Breitkopf & Härtel edition. 192pp. 9 × 12. 25125-X Pa. **$10.95**

SELECTED SONGS FOR SOLO VOICE AND PIANO, Robert Schumann. Over 100 of Schumann's greatest lieder, set to poems by Heine, Goethe, Byron, others. Breitkopf & Härtel edition. 248pp. 9⅜ × 12¼. 24202-1 Pa. **$13.95**

THIRTY SONGS, Franz Liszt. Selection of extremely worthwhile though not widely-known songs. Texts in French, German, and Italian, all with English translations. Piano, high voice. 144pp. 9 × 12. 23197-6 Pa. **$9.95**

OFFENBACH'S SONGS FROM THE GREAT OPERETTAS, Jacques Offenbach. Piano, vocal (French text) for 38 most popular songs: *Orphée, Belle Héléne, Vie Parisienne, Duchesse de Gérolstein,* others. 21 illustrations. 195pp. 9 × 12. 23341-3 Pa. **$12.95**

SONGS, 1880–1904, Claude Debussy. Rich selection of 36 songs set to texts by Verlaine, Baudelaire, Pierre Louÿs, Charles d'Orleans, others. 175pp. 9 × 12. 24131-9 Pa. **$9.95**

THE COMPLETE MÖRIKE SONGS, Hugo Wolf. Splendid settings of 53 poems by Eduard Mörike. "Der Tambour," "Elfenlied," "Verborganheit," 50 more. New prose translations. 208pp. 9⅜ × 12¼. 24380-X Pa. **$11.95**

SPANISH AND ITALIAN SONGBOOKS, Hugo Wolf. Total of 90 songs by great 19th-century master of the genre. Reprint of authoritative C. F. Peters edition. New Translations of German texts. 256pp. 9⅜ × 12¼. 26156-5 Pa. **$13.95**

SIXTY SONGS, Gabriel Fauré. "Clair de lune," "Apres un reve," "Chanson du pecheur," "Automne," and other great songs set for medium voice. Reprinted from French editions. 288pp. 8⅜ × 11. (Not available in France or Germany) 26534-X Pa. **$14.95**

FRENCH ART SONGS OF THE NINETEENTH-CENTURY, Philip Hale (ed.). 39 songs from romantic period by 18 composers: Berlioz, Chausson, Debussy (six songs), Gounod, Massenet, Thomas, etc. For high voice, French text, English singing translation. 182pp. 9 × 12. (Not available in France or Germany) 23680-3 Pa. **$11.95**

COMPLETE SONGS FOR SOLO VOICE AND PIANO (two volumes), Johannes Brahms. A total of 113 songs in complete score by greatest lieder writer since Schubert. Volume I contains 15-song cycle Die Schone Magelone; Volume II famous "Lullaby." Total of 448pp. 9⅜ × 12¼.
Volume I 23820-2 Pa. **$12.95**
Volume II 23821-0 Pa. **$12.95**

COMPLETE SONGS FOR SOLO VOICE AND PIANO: Series III, Johannes Brahms. 64 songs, published between 1877–86, including such favorites as "Geheimnis," "Alte Liebe," and "Vergebliches Standchen." 224pp. 9 × 12. 23822-9 Pa. **$12.95**

COMPLETE SONGS FOR SOLO VOICE AND PIANO: Series IV, Johannes Brahms. 120 songs that complete the Brahms song oeuvre and sensitive arrangements of 91 folk and traditional songs. 240pp. 9 × 12. 23823-7 Pa. **$12.95**

---

*Available from your music dealer or write for **free** Music Catalog to*
Dover Publications, Inc., Dept. MUBI, 31 East 2nd Street, Mineola, N.Y. 11501.